Legendary Customer Service

GEMS MASTERY SERIES

HOW TO THRIVE IN AMERICA DURING TOUGH ECONOMIC TIMES

Quotes Compiled & Edited

by

DeCarlo A. Eskridge

NU DAE Enterprise Publications

United States of America

ISBN-13: 978-1469912790
ISBN-10: 1469912791

Edited by DeCarlo A. Eskridge
Cover Design ©NU DAE Enterprises, LLC, 2012
DeCarloEskridge.com

Printed in the United States of America

To my grandchildren
Mikey, Micah, Jaden, and Amari

Acknowledgments

Jesus (1), Will Rogers (2), Nelson Boswell (3, 59), Jeff
Bezos (4, 54), Sam Walton (5), Bill Gates (7), Walt Disney
(8), Charles Darwin (9), Brigade Ad (10), Brian Tracy (11,
63), Robert Bowman (12), William Paley (13), PeopleSoft
Ad (14, 68), Benjamin Franklin (15, 62), Kate Zabriskie
(16, 70, 97), Laurie McIntosh (17), Horst Schulz (18),
DeCarlo A. Eskridge (19, 73,121), Peter Drucker (20, 61,
106), Robert Gately (21), Siebel ad (22), Donald Porter
(23), Tom Watson (25, 94), Kevin Stirtz (26, 93), Mark
Perrault (27), Schwieters Companies, Inc. (28), David
Seabury (29), Stew Leonard (30), Jeffrey Gitomer (31, 58,
92), Gary Comer (33), Napoleon Hill (34), Tom Reilly
(35), S. Parkes Cadma (36), Robert Greenleaf (37), Albert
Einstein (38), Heather Williams (39), Howard Schultz (40),
Elbert Hubbard (41), Zig Ziglar (42), Tom Peters (44),
Michael LeBoeuf (45), Leon Gorman (46), Gene Buckley
(47), Ray Krock (48), John Mackey (49), Henry Ford (50),
Mother Teresa (51), Ross Perot (53), Ben Cohen (55), John
Russell (56), Steve Jobs (57), J. C. Penney (60), Jerry Yang
(64), Betsy Sanders (65), Judy Silva (67), Alice
Macdougall (69), Socrates (71), Claus Moller (72), Jerry
Gregoire (74), Giorgio Armani (75), Tony Allesandra (76),
Lewis Carol (77), John Adams (78), Jan Carlzon (79),
Booker T. Washington (80), Doug Warner (81), Chip Bell
(82), Dale Carnegie (83), Mahatma Gandhi (84), Katherine
Barchetti (85), Mark Cuban (86), John Ilhan (88), Jerry
Fritz (89), James Joyce (90), Brown & Williamson
Tobacco Ad (91), Rick Tate (95), Richard Bach (96),
Arthur F. Sheldon (98), Marshall Field (99), Damon
Richards (100), Nigel Sanders (101), Samuel Taylor
Coleridge (103), Toby Bloomberg (104), Robert Half (105),

William H. Davidow (107), W. Edwards Deming (108), Shiv Singh (109), Sally Gronow (110), David Yu (111), Martin Oliver (112), Stephen Covey (113), Laura Ashley (114), Doug Smith (115), Rita De Acosta Lydig (116), Penny Handscomb (117), Kees Kamies (118), Graham Day (119), C. F. Norton (120), Eleanor Roosevelt (123), Norman Vincent Peale (124), W. E. Channing (125)

Introduction

If we are to get America back to work, it is imperative that we return to the values that made this nation great. There is a common thread among all thriving companies. They all understand the importance of customer service excellence. Legendary customer service begins with a commitment to the customer... at any cost!

In order to differentiate from your competition, you must stop talking about customer service excellence and start living it. This ideology must flow from the pinnacle of your organization to the very core of its foundation - persons who interact directly with your customers on a daily basis. A positive customer encounter can change the customer's perception of your organization from ordinary to exceptional. Therefore, it is paramount to understand that your organization's success depends entirely on its ability to create positive and memorable customer service experiences.

In this book, you will discover timeless gems (*quotes*) from some of the world's most influential leaders. Leaders and innovators, who have turned their values into action and, in the process, changed the way the world does business. This book is required reading for all who work with and/or support customers. In order to get the most from your reading, we recommend that you read **Legendary Customer Service** until you master the precious gems within.

$\mathcal{T}$reat people the same way you want them to treat you.

- Jesus

You never get a second chance to make a good first impression.

- Will Rogers

♦

$\mathcal{H}$ere is a simple but powerful rule: always give people more than what they expect to get.

- Nelson Boswell

♦

$\mathcal{I}$f you make customers unhappy in the physical world, they might each tell 6 friends.
If you make customers unhappy on the Internet, they can each tell 6,000 friends.

- **Jeff Bezos**

$\mathcal{T}$he goal as a company is to have customer service that is not just the best but legendary.

- Sam Walton

◆

The quality of your work
depends on the quality of
your people.

- Anonymous

♦

*Y*our most unhappy customers are your greatest source of learning.

- Bill Gates

◆

$\mathcal{D}$o what you do so well that they will want to see it again and bring their friends.

- Walt Disney

◆

It is not the strongest of the species that survives, nor the most intelligent, but the one most responsive to change.

- Charles Darwin

♦

$\mathcal{C}$ustomers who don't get support become someone else' customers.

- **Brigade Ad**

*Y*our earning ability today is largely dependent upon your knowledge, skill and your ability to combine that knowledge and skill in such a way that you contribute value for which customers are going to pay.

- Brian Tracy

♦

$\mathcal{W}$hatever your business is, talk to your customers and provide them with what they want. It makes sense.

- Robert Bowman

♦

What we are doing is satisfying the American public. That is our job. I always say we have to give most of the people what they want most of the time. That is what is expected of us.

- William Paley

◆

$\mathcal{C}$ustomer service is training people how to serve clients in an outstanding fashion.

- PeopleSoft Ad

◆

$\mathcal{W}$ell done is better than well said.

- Benjamin Franklin

♦

When you start viewing your customers as interruptions, you're going to have problems.

- Kate Zabriskie

♦

You are serving a customer, not a life sentence. Learn how to enjoy your work.

- Laurie McIntosh

♦

*U*nless you have 100% customer satisfaction … you must improve.

- Horst Schulz

◆

*O*utstanding customer service is a combination of little things working together.

- DeCarlo A. Eskridge

Quality in a service or product is not what you put into it. It is what the client or customer gets out of it.

- Peter Drucker

♦

People expect good service but few are willing to give it.

- Robert Gately

♦

Good service is good
business.

- Siebel ad

◆

$\mathscr{C}$ustomers don't expect you to be perfect. They do expect you to fix things when they go wrong.

- Donald Porter

◆

Perceived quality is based on what the customer expects.

- Anonymous

◆

If you don't genuinely like your customers, chances are they won't buy.

- Tom Watson

◆

*K*now what your customers want most and what your company does best. Focus on where those two meet.

- Kevin Stirtz

♦

$\mathscr{O}$f the shopper feels like it was poor service, then it was poor service. We are in the customer perception business.

- Mark Perrault

◆

The customer is our reason for being here.

- Schwieters Companies, Inc.

◆

$\mathscr{N}$othing that is weak
continues to serve.

- David Seabury

◆

Rule 1: The customer is always right.
Rule 2: If the customer is ever wrong, re-read Rule 1.

- Stew Leonard

◆

$\mathcal{B}$iggest question: Isn't it really 'customer helping' rather than customer service? And wouldn't you deliver better service if you thought of it that way?

- Jeffrey Gitomer

♦

People perform best and deliver the best customer service when they like what they do.

- Anonymous

◆

$\mathcal{W}$orry about being
better; bigger will take
care of itself. Think one
customer at a time and take
care of each one the best
way you can.

- Gary Comer

♦

$\mathcal{O}$ne of the most important principles of success is developing the habit of going the extra mile.

- Napoleon Hill

◆

$\mathcal{C}$ustomer service is more
than a department,
it's an attitude!

- **Tom Reilly**

$\mathcal{A}$ little experience often upsets a lot of theory.

- S. Parkes Cadma

◆

$\mathcal{G}$ood leaders must first become good servants.

- Robert Greenleaf

$\mathcal{O}$nly a life lived in the service to others is worth living.

- Albert Einstein

$\mathcal{R}$evolve your world
around the customer and
more customers will
revolve around you.

- Heather Williams

◆

$\mathcal{O}$ur mission statement about treating people with respect and dignity is not just words but a creed we live by every day. You can't expect your employees to exceed the expectations of your customers if you don't exceed the employees' expectations of management.

- Howard Schultz

◆

$\mathcal{M}$en are rich only as they give. He who gives great service gets great rewards.

- Elbert Hubbard

◆

$\mathcal{S}$tatistics suggest that when customers complain, business owners and managers ought to get excited about it. The complaining customer represents a huge opportunity for more business.

- **Zig Ziglar**

♦

*Treat every customer
as if they sign your
paycheck …
because they do.*

- Anonymous

◆

$\mathcal{E}$xcellent firms don't believe in excellence – only in constant improvement and constant change.

- **Tom Peters**

◆

Every company's greatest assets are its customers, because without customers there is no company.

- Michael LeBoeuf

♦

*C*ustomer service is just a day in, day out ongoing, never ending, unremitting, persevering, compassionate, type of activity.

- Leon Gorman

♦

Don't try to tell the customer what he wants. If you want to be smart, be smart in the shower. Then get out, go to work and serve the customer!

- Gene Buckley

♦

$\mathcal{O}f$ you work just for money, you'll never make it, but if you love what you're doing and you always put the customer first, success will be yours.

- Ray Krock

◆

For us, our most
important stakeholder is
not our stockholders,
it is our customers.
We're in business
to serve the needs and
desires of our core
customer base.

- John Mackey

◆

$\mathcal{I}$t is not the employer who pays the wages. Employers only handle the money. It is the customer who pays the wages.

- Henry Ford

$\mathcal{K}$ind words can be short and easy to speak, but their echoes are truly endless.

- Mother Teresa

♦

$\mathcal{M}$ake 'heroes' out of people who deliver the best customer service.

- Anonymous

◆

$\mathcal{S}$pend a lot of time talking to customers face to face. You'd be amazed how many companies don't listen to their customers.

- Ross Perot

◆

$\mathcal{I}$f you do build a great experience, customers tell each other about that. Word of mouth is very powerful.

- Jeff Bezos

♦

$\mathcal{T}$here is a spiritual aspect to our lives – when we give we receive – when a business does something good for somebody, that somebody feels good about them!

- Ben Cohen

♦

The more you engage with customers the clearer things become and the easier it is to determine what you should be doing.

- John Russell

◆

$\mathcal{A}$ lot of companies have chosen to downsize, and maybe that was the right thing for them. We chose a different path. Our belief was that if we kept putting great products in front of customers, they would continue to open their wallets.

- Steve Jobs

♦

*C*ustomer satisfaction is worthless. Customer loyalty is priceless.

- Jeffrey Gitomer

♦

*H*ere is a simple but powerful rule: always give people more than what they expect to get.

- Nelson Boswell

♦

Every great business is
built on friendship.

- J.C. Penney

♦

The purpose of business is to create and keep a customer.

- Peter Drucker

The bitterness of poor quality
quality
lingers long after the
sweetness of a low price is
forgotten.

- Benjamin Franklin

◆

$\mathcal{C}$ustomers today want the very most and the very best for the very least amount of money, and on the best terms. Only the individuals and companies that provide absolutely excellent products and services at absolutely excellent prices will survive.

- Brian Tracy

♦

$\mathcal{I}$t helps a ton when you learn people's names and don't butcher them when trying to pronounce them.

- Jerry Yang

◆

Service, in short, is not what you do, but who you are. It is a way of living that you need to bring to everything you do, if you are to bring it to your customer interactions

- **Betsy Sanders**

♦

$\mathcal{M}$ake it a 'joy' for people to do business with you.

- Anonymous

◆

To my customer:
I may not have the answer,
but I'll find it.
I may not have the time,
but I'll make it. I may not
be the biggest, but I'll be
the most committed to
your success.

- Judy Silva

♦

*C*ustomers are an investment. Maximize your return.

- PeopleSoft Ad

$\mathcal{O}$n business you get what you want by giving other people what they want.

- Alice Macdougall

♦

Although your customers won't love you if you give bad service, your competitors will.

- Kate Zabriskie

$\mathcal{T}$he way to gain a good
reputation,
is to endeavor to be what
you desire to appear.

- Socrates

◆

A complaint is a gift.

- Claus Moller

◆

$\mathcal{T}$o understand your customer, you must first walk a mile in her stilettos.

- DeCarlo A. Eskridge

♦

The customer experience is the next competitive battleground.

- Jerry Gregoire

$\mathcal{I}$n the end, the customer doesn't know, or care, if you are small or large as an organization. She or he only focuses on the garment hanging on the rail in the store.

- Giorgio Armani

♦

Being on par in terms of price and quality only gets you into the game. Service wins the game.

- Tony Allesandra

♦

$\mathcal{O}$ne of the deep secrets
of life is that all that is
really worth doing is what
we do for others.

- Lewis Carol

♦

$\mathcal{I}$f we do not lay out ourselves in the service of mankind whom should we serve?

- John Adams

♦

$\mathcal{I}$f you're not serving the customer, your job is to be serving someone who is.

- Jan Carlzon

♦

$\mathscr{O}$f you want to lift
yourself up,
lift up
someone else.

- Booker T. Washington

◆

$\mathcal{O}$n the world of Internet Customer Service, it's important to remember your competitor is only one mouse click away.

- Doug Warner

♦

*L*oyal customers, they don't just come back, they don't simply recommend you, they insist that their friends do business with you.

- Chip Bell

♦

$\mathcal{D}$ealing with people is probably the biggest problem you face, especially if you are in business. Yes, and that is also true if you are a housewife, architect or engineer.

- Dale Carnegie

♦

$\mathcal{A}$ customer is the most important visitor on our premises, he is not dependent on us. We are dependent on him. He is not an interruption in our work. He is the purpose of it. He is not an outsider in our business. He is part of it. We are not doing him a favor by serving him. He is doing us a favor by giving us an opportunity to do so.

- Mahatma Gandhi

◆

84

*M*ake a customer,
not a sale.

- Katherine Barchetti

◆

$\mathcal{M}$ake your product easier to buy than your competition, or you will find your customers buying from them, not you.

- **Mark Cuban**

♦

$\mathscr{C}$ontinually look for ways to improve quality and add value to products your customers purchase.

- Anonymous

◆

It's a very, very tough market. So unless you do a really good job, you buy the right products from the manufacturers, you service the customer, they keep coming back, they bring their friends in, it's all about numbers, numbers, numbers.

- John Ilhan

♦

You'll never have a product or price advantage again. They can be easily duplicated, but a strong customer service culture can't be copied.

- Jerry Fritz

♦

Mistakes are the portals
of discovery.

- James Joyce

◆

I won't complain.
I just won't come back.

- Brown & Williamson Tobacco Ad

$\mathscr{F}$riendly makes sales –
and friendly generates
repeat business.

- Jeffrey Gitomer

◆

Every contact we have with a customer influences whether or not they'll come back. We have to be great every time or we'll lose them.

- Kevin Stirtz

◆

$\mathcal{I}$f you don't genuinely like your customers, chances are they won't buy.

- **Tom Watson**

$\mathcal{M}$erely satisfying customers will not be enough to earn their loyalty. Instead, they must experience exceptional service worthy of their repeat business and referral. Understand the factors that drive this customer revolution.

- Rick Tate

◆

$\mathcal{I}$ don't do business with those who don't make a profit because they can't give the best service.

- Richard Bach

♦

The customer's
perception is your reality.

- Kate Zabriskie

$\mathcal{H}$e profits, most who
serves best.

- Arthur F. Sheldon

$\mathcal{R}$ight or wrong,
the customer is always
right.

- Marshall Field

Your customer doesn't care how much you know until they know how much you care.

- Damon Richards

◆

Every client you keep,
is one less that you need to
find.

- Nigel Sanders

*N*ever be the reason a customer doesn't come back.

- Anonymous

◆

Nothing is so contagious as enthusiasm.

- Samuel Taylor Coleridge

◆

$\mathcal{U}$nder promise and over deliver.

- Toby Bloomberg

When the customer comes first, the customer will last.

- Robert Half

The single most important thing to remember about any enterprise is that there are no results inside its walls. The result of a business is a satisfied customer.

- Peter Drucker

♦

The longer you wait, the harder it is to produce outstanding customer service.

- **William H. Davidow**

Profit in business comes from repeat customers; customers that boast about your product and service, and that bring friends with them.

- W. Edwards Deming

♦

The purpose of a business is to create a customer who creates customers.

- Shiv Singh

♦

$\mathcal{G}$ood customer service
costs less than bad
customer service.

- Sally Gronow

◆

It's much harder to provide a great customer service than I would have ever realized. It's much more art than science in some of these other areas and not just about the facts but about how you are conveying them.

- David Yu

♦

$\mathcal{W}$hether you are big or small, you cannot give good customer service if your employees don't feel good about coming to work.

- Martin Oliver

♦

If we keep doing what we're doing, we're going to keep getting what we're getting.

- Stephen Covey

♦

$\mathcal{W}$e don't want to push
our ideas on to
customers, we simply want
to make what they want.

- Laura Ashley

♦

It starts with respect.
If you respect the
customer as a human
being, and truly honor their
right to be treated fairly
and honestly,
everything else is much
easier.

- Doug Smith

♦

$\mathcal{A}$ shoe without sex appeal is like a tree without leaves. Service without emotion is like a shoe without sex appeal.

- **Rita De Acosta Lydig**

◆

$\mathcal{E}$veryone in an organization should be involved with customer service, not only are they feeling the customer but they are getting a feeling for what's not working.

- Penny Handscomb

♦

Give trust, and you'll get
it double in return

- Kees Kamies

♦

$\mathcal{I}$f you love your customer to death, you can't go wrong.

- Graham Day

♦

$\mathscr{N}$othing is ever gained
by winning an argument
and losing a customer.

- C. F. Norton

◆

Satisfied customers purchase either 'good feelings' or 'solutions to problems' endeavor to give them both.

- DeCarlo A. Eskridge

◆

Make it easy for people to buy from you.

- Anonymous

◆

$\mathcal{I}$t is not fair to ask of
others what you are not
willing to do yourself.

- Eleanor Roosevelt

◆

Of you paint in your mind a picture of bright and happy expectations, you put yourself into a condition conductive to your goal.

- Norman Vincent Peale

♦

$\mathcal{F}$ix your eyes on perfection and you make almost everything speed towards it.

- W. E. Channing

♦

About the Author

DeCarlo A. Eskridge is a spiritual life-coach/ trainer, host of Blogtalk Radio's "Live Your Greatness," motivational speaker, certified hypnotherapist, certified N.L.P. practitioner/ trainer, author, and minister. He is very proud to have authored and independently-published several books through his company NU DAE Enterprises where he serves as President and CEO.

A prolific teacher and encourager, DeCarlo A. Eskridge reads over 50 books a year, and listens to countless hours of audio programs. He is a Certified Life Coach through Franklin Covey and a motivational speaker who earned advanced honors at Toastmasters International. He is also an Ordained Minister with over 25 years of biblical study.

DeCarlo A. Eskridge has been imbued with an inexhaustible, unyielding, and unrelenting thirst and hunger for knowledge. His mission is to travel the globe teaching, empowering, inspiring, and transforming the lives of millions with the truths he has discovered in order that every person recognizes who he or she is, what he or she can accomplish, and that they live it!

GEMS MASTERY SERIES

NU DAE Enterprise Publications

DeCarloEskridge.com

ISBN-13: 978-1469912790
ISBN-10: 1469912791